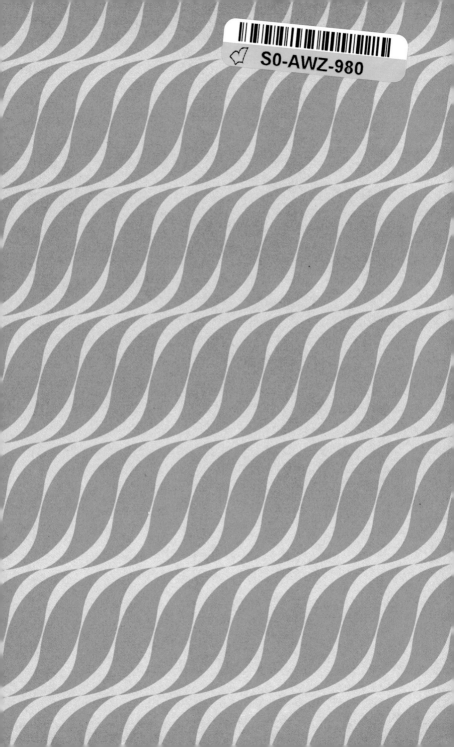

RECIPES
KIDS CAN
COOK

Consulting Editor:
Valerie Ferguson

southwater

Contents

Introduction

Cooking is fun and surprisingly easy. You will soon discover that serving and eating something that you have cooked yourself makes you feel really special—and it will also be a treat for the rest of the family.

There are lots of favorite recipes for all types of food—savory and sweet—and some new dishes and cakes to try. Some of them are very easy and quick and, if you have never cooked anything before, these are the best ones to start with. Other recipes might look a little more difficult, but actually just take a bit longer.

Before you start, it's a good idea to read the first part of this book. This explains what to do and what not to do to be safe in the kitchen, and these rules apply just as much to grown-ups. Then there is some helpful information about equipment. This is followed by an A–Z guide to cooking terms and some helpful techniques.

The rest of the book is the fun part with five chapters of recipes, which include snacks, cakes and cookies, as well as all the courses of a meal from soups and appetizers to desserts. Lots of different techniques are used, so you will be learning new and very useful skills all the time. So get out the pots and pans and enjoy yourself.

Safety & Getting Started

The kitchen is full of things that could be very dangerous, such as electric sockets, hot ovens and stoves, fast-moving equipment and hot pans. It's therefore very important that you take as much care as possible.

Tie long hair back—then it can't get caught on equipment, will keep away from flames and won't become an extra ingredient in your recipe!

Always wash your hands—not just when you begin to cook but as you handle different ingredients. When handling raw meat, it's important not to touch any ingredients that aren't going to be cooked.

Water and electricity don't mix, so dry your hands before touching any sockets or plugging in machinery. Make sure you switch off before pulling out the plug.

Read through the recipe before you start. Have everything ready: panic causes problems! Protect your clothes and roll up those sleeves!

Is the work surface too high? Making pastry or cakes means working in a mixing bowl, and it might be hard to get your hands right in there. Put the bowl on the kitchen table or stand it in the empty sink instead, as both these places are much lower than a kitchen work surface.

Always use oven mitts or a thickly folded, dry dish towel (wet ones let the heat through) to lift things in and out of the oven. If a dish is too heavy to lift out of a hot oven or from one surface to another, ask a grown-up to help. Keep saucepan handles away from any heat source and check that they aren't hot before trying to lift the pan.

Some recipes call for hot liquids and foods to be drained or poured into something else. Please do this extremely carefully. Don't overfill the pan and, if it's too heavy or you aren't sure you can manage, ask a grown-up for some help.

Wipe up any wet spills on the floor, especially oil, at once. Use hot, soapy water and then rub the area dry so the floor doesn't become a skating rink.

All this is not really complicated: it's a matter of being careful and sensible and thinking about what you are doing. Remember that most accidents happen in the home: make sure you aren't one of them!

Equipment

All cooking jobs in the kitchen need a tool of some sort, although a few basic ones can do most jobs. If you are in any doubt about which piece of equipment to use or how to use it, ask a grown-up.

Ovens: There are lots of different types, using different sorts of energy, and each one has its own temperature guide.. To preheat the oven will take about 10 minutes. If you put the food in before the oven is hot enough, it will take longer to cook, and some food will not cook correctly.

Cutting Boards: If you chop onions or garlic, wash the board well, or use a separate board so the strong flavors don't affect other foods.

Graters: A pyramid- or box-shaped grater is the most useful type. Each side has a different grating surface.

Bowls: Mixing bowls come in all sizes, and the most useful are made from heatproof glass.

Pans: Saucepans and frying pans can be made from different materials. The most popular are aluminum and stainless steel.

Spatula: This is not just useful for lifting and turning fish, but also burgers or even eggs!

Knives: Everyone knows that knives must be used carefully, but it's easy to get careless. Pick the right size for the job and try not to be distracted.

Whisk: A whisk's main function is to beat in air and make the mixture bigger and thicker. It can also blend things together and make them smooth, such as sauces.

Wooden Spoons: These come in various lengths. Short ones are best for beating cake mixtures, but ones with longer handles are better for cooking on the stove because your hand is farther from the heat.

Cooking Terms

Sometimes cooking terms seem like a foreign language, with lots of words you aren't sure about. Hopefully this guide will explain most of them.

Bake: To cook in the oven, in dry heat, at a set temperature.

Blend: To mix ingredients evenly. Also describes the action of a blender.

Boil: A liquid is boiling when the edges are rolling over and large bubbles are heaving on the surface.

Brown: Meat and vegetables are often browned by frying at the start of a recipe, to give a good, even color and a more savory flavor.

Core: To cut out the tough central part and seeds of a fruit.

Cream: To beat fat (usually butter or margarine) and sugar together until they are light and fluffy.

Fold In: To add something to a mixture very gently, so as not to break up all the air bubbles, such as folding flour into a cake mixture.

Fry: To cook food in hot fat or oil to get a crisp, browned outer surface.

Garnish: To decorate savory food with herbs or chopped vegetables.

Grate: To shred into tiny strips using a grater.

Grease: Brushing cooking pans or baking sheets with oil or margarine helps to prevent food from sticking.

Purée: To turn soft, solid food into a smoother, thicker food.

Sieve: To shake dry foods through a sieve to remove any lumps.

Simmer: To reduce the heat once the liquid has come to a boil so it still bubbles lightly.

Whisk: To mix air into egg whites or yolks and other ingredients with a hand-held whisk or electric beater.

Techniques

Preparing Onions

Chopping the onions to a similar size means they all cook at the same time, but don't slice your fingers as well!

1 Cut the onion in half with the skin still on. Lie the cut-side flat on a board. Trim off both ends. Peel off the skin. Make several parallel cuts lengthwise (from trimmed end to end), but not cutting right to one end.

2 Make cuts at right angles to the first ones, at the same distance apart. Finally, chop the end.

COOK'S TIP: When an onion is described as "sliced," cut through each half to make vertical slices.

Preparing Carrots

Although they are often just sliced in circles, carrots can look much more attractive cut in a different way.

1 Peel the carrot, using a swivel peeler, and trim the ends.

2 Cut the carrot into short lengths and then into thin slices, lengthwise. You will need a sharp knife for this job, so be careful.

3 Cut each thin slice into fine strips, about the size of matchsticks.

COOK'S TIP: Use tiny cutters to stamp out shapes from the thin slices, to garnish soups or salads.

Super-duper Soup

Easy to make, as there's no need to be too fussy—just chop up lots of your favorite vegetables and simmer them gently with tomatoes and stock.

Serves 4–6

INGREDIENTS

1 tablespoon oil
1 onion, sliced
2 carrots, sliced
1½ pounds potatoes, cut in large chunks
5 cups vegetable stock
1-pound can chopped tomatoes
4 ounces broccoli, cut into florets
1 zucchini, sliced
1⅓ cups mushrooms, sliced
1½ teaspoons medium-hot curry
  powder (optional)
1 teaspoon dried mixed herbs
salt and freshly ground black pepper

1 Heat the oil in a large saucepan and sauté the onion and carrots gently, until they start to soften.

2 Add the potatoes and cook gently for 2 more minutes; stir often or they might stick. Add the stock, tomatoes, broccoli, zucchini and mushrooms.

3 Add the curry powder (if using), herbs and a little salt and pepper and bring to a boil. Put the lid on and simmer gently for 30–40 minutes or until the vegetables are tender. Taste the soup and add more salt and pepper if needed.

Corn & Potato Chowder

This hearty and substantial soup is wonderful served with thick crusty bread and topped with melted Cheddar cheese.

Serves 4

INGREDIENTS
1 onion, chopped
1 garlic clove, crushed
1 medium potato, chopped
2 celery stalks, sliced
1 small green bell pepper, seeded,
   halved and sliced
2 tablespoons sunflower oil
2 tablespoons butter
2½ cups vegetable stock
   or water
1¼ cups milk
7-ounce can lima beans
11-ounce can corn
pinch of dried sage
salt and freshly ground black pepper

1 Put the onion, garlic, potato, celery and green pepper into a large saucepan with the oil and butter. Heat the ingredients until sizzling, then turn the heat down to low. Cover and cook the vegetables gently for 10 minutes, shaking the pan occasionally.

2 Pour in the stock or water, add a little salt and pepper and bring to a boil. Turn down the heat, cover and simmer gently for about 15 minutes.

3 Add the milk, beans and corn— including the juice from the cans— and the sage. Simmer again for 5 minutes. Taste and add more salt and pepper if needed and serve hot.

Crispy Hot Dogs

Instead of putting the frankfurters in rolls, they are wrapped in slices of bread and baked.

Makes 8

INGREDIENTS
8 slices white or brown bread,
   crusts cut off
¼ cup soft margarine
1 tablespoon German mustard
8 frankfurters
tomato wedges and fresh
   flat-leaf parsley,
   to garnish
sauerkraut, to serve

1 Preheat the oven to 400°F. Flatten the bread slices lightly with a rolling pin so that they roll up more easily.

2 Spread the slices of bread with a little margarine, and then spread them with mustard.

3 Place a frankfurter diagonally across each slice of bread and roll up tightly, holding it in place with a toothpick. Spread each roll with margarine and place on a baking sheet. Bake for 15–20 minutes, until the bread is golden.

4 Meanwhile, heat the sauerkraut in a saucepan. Remove the toothpicks from the hot dogs and serve with hot sauerkraut and a garnish of tomato wedges and flat-leaf parsley.

Eggs in Nests

Part of the fun with cooking is to make dishes look attractive, so that everyone really looks forward to eating them.

Serves 4

INGREDIENTS
4 large baking potatoes
3 tablespoons butter
2 tablespoons hot light cream
   or milk
2 tablespoons snipped
   fresh chives
4 eggs
about ½ cup finely grated
   Cheddar cheese
salt and freshly ground
   black pepper

1 Preheat the oven to 400°F. Bake the potatoes for about 1½ hours, until soft.

2 Lay each potato on its side and cut off a slice about a quarter of the way down. Scoop the flesh into a bowl, taking care not to make a hole in the skins.

3 Add the butter, cream or milk, chives and a little salt and pepper to the bowl and mash together.

4 Divide the potato mixture among the potato skins, and make a dip in each with the back of a spoon. Break an egg into each dip, then return to the oven for about 10 minutes, until the eggs are just set. Sprinkle the cheese on the eggs, then place under the broiler until golden.

Cheesy Mashed Potato Patties

Using up leftovers in a clever way is a useful skill to learn—and it saves money.

Serves 4

INGREDIENTS
5 cups mashed potatoes
8 ounces cooked cabbage, shredded
1 egg, beaten
1 cup Cheddar cheese, grated
pinch of grated fresh nutmeg
all-purpose flour, for coating
vegetable oil, for frying
salt and freshly ground black pepper

1 Mix the potatoes with the cabbage, egg, cheese, nutmeg and a little salt and pepper. Divide the mixture into eight equal pieces and shape them into patties.

2 Chill in the refrigerator for an hour or so, if possible, as this helps the mixture to become firm and makes it easier to fry. Dip the patties in the flour. Heat about ½ inch of oil in a frying pan until it is quite hot.

3 Carefully slide the patties into the oil and fry on each side for about 3 minutes, until golden and crisp. Drain on paper towels and serve hot and crisp.

Cheese & Chutney Toasts

Cheese melted on toast can be made quite memorable with a few tasty additions.

Serves 4

INGREDIENTS
4 thick slices whole-wheat bread
butter, for spreading
1 cup Cheddar cheese, grated
1 teaspoon dried thyme
2 tablespoons chutney
   or relish
freshly ground black pepper
salad, to serve

1 Toast the bread slices lightly on each side, then spread sparingly with butter.

2 Mix the grated cheese and thyme together and add a little pepper.

3 Spread the chutney or relish on the toast and divide the cheese equally among the four slices.

4 Return the slices to the broiler and cook until browned and bubbling. Cut into halves, diagonally, and serve with salad.

Right: Cheesy Mashed Potato Patties (top); Cheese & Chutney Toasts

Peanut Butter Fingers

These popular crispy treats are very easy to make and even easier to eat, so be sure you make enough.

Makes 12

INGREDIENTS
2¼ pounds potatoes
1 large onion, chopped
2 large bell peppers, red or green, seeded
   and chopped
3 carrots, coarsely grated
3 tablespoons sunflower oil
2 zucchini, coarsely grated
1½ cups mushrooms, chopped
1 tablespoon dried mixed herbs
1 cup Cheddar cheese, grated
½ cup crunchy peanut butter
2 eggs, beaten
about ½ cup dried bread crumbs
3 tablespoons Parmesan
   cheese, grated
vegetable oil, for frying
salt and freshly ground
   black pepper
salad, to serve

3 Combine the potato, onion mixture, mixed herbs, grated cheese and peanut butter. Add a little salt and pepper, let cool for 30 minutes, then stir in one of the eggs.

4 Spread the mixture out on a large plate, cool and chill in the refrigerator. Divide into 12 portions and shape into "sausages." Dip your hands in cold water if the mixture sticks.

1 Boil the potatoes for about 20 minutes, until tender, then drain well and mash. Set aside.

2 Sauté the onion, peppers and carrots gently in the sunflower oil for about 5 minutes, then add the zucchini and mushrooms. Cook for 5 more minutes.

5 Put the second egg in a bowl and dip the potato fingers into it first, then into the crumbs and Parmesan cheese until coated evenly. Return to the refrigerator to set.

6 Heat about ½ inch vegetable oil in a large frying pan. Carefully add the fingers and cook, turning frequently, for 4–5 minutes, until golden all over. If there is not room for all the fingers at once, cook them in two or three separate batches. Drain on paper towels and serve hot with salad.

COOK'S TIP: You might find it easier to beat the two eggs in separate bowls, as you will need them at different stages in the recipe.

Hummus

This nutritious dip can be served with raw vegetable sticks or packed into salad-filled pitas, but it is best spread thickly on hot buttered toast.

Serves 4

INGREDIENTS
14-ounce can chickpeas, drained
2 garlic cloves
2 tablespoons tahini or smooth
    peanut butter
¼ cup olive oil
juice of 1 lemon
½ teaspoon cayenne pepper
1 tablespoon sesame seeds
sea salt

1 Rinse the chickpeas well and place in a blender or food processor with the garlic and a good pinch of sea salt. Process until very finely chopped.

COOK'S TIP: Tahini is a thick, smooth and oily paste made from sesame seeds. It is available at health-food stores and large supermarkets. Peanut butter would not be used in a traditional recipe, but it is a useful substitute.

2 Add the tahini or peanut butter and process until fairly smooth. With the motor still running, slowly pour in the oil and lemon juice.

3 Stir in the cayenne pepper and add more salt, to taste. If the mixture is too thick, stir in a little cold water. Transfer the purée to a serving bowl.

4 Heat a small nonstick pan and add the sesame seeds. Cook them for 2–3 minutes, shaking the pan, until the seeds are golden. Let cool, then sprinkle them on the purée.

Spanish Omelet

Spanish omelet belongs in every cook's repertoire and can vary according to what ingredients you have in your pantry. This version includes soft white beans.

Serves 4

INGREDIENTS
2 tablespoons olive oil
1 teaspoon sesame oil
1 Spanish onion, chopped
1 small red bell pepper, seeded and diced
2 celery stalks, chopped
14-ounce can soft white
    beans, drained
8 eggs
3 tablespoons sesame seeds
salt and freshly ground black pepper
green salad, to serve

2 Add the beans and continue to cook gently, stirring occasionally for several minutes, to heat through.

3 In a small bowl beat the eggs with a fork, add a little salt and pepper and pour onto the ingredients in the pan.

4 Stir the egg mixture with a flat wooden spoon until it begins to stiffen, then let become firm over low heat for 6–8 minutes.

1 Heat the olive and sesame oils in a large frying pan. Add the onion, pepper and celery and cook them for 3–5 minutes, to soften but not color.

VARIATION: You can also use sliced cooked potatoes, any seasonal vegetables, baby artichoke hearts and chickpeas in a Spanish omelet.

5 Preheat a medium broiler. Sprinkle the omelet with sesame seeds and brown evenly under the broiler.

6 Cut the omelet into thick wedges and serve warm with a green salad.

Pasta Spirals with Pepperoni & Tomato Sauce

You can use any pasta shapes for this dish—they are all cooked the same way.

Serves 4

INGREDIENTS
1 medium onion
1 red bell pepper
1 green bell pepper
2 tablespoons olive oil, plus extra for
    tossing the pasta
1¾ pounds canned chopped tomatoes
2 tablespoons tomato paste
2 teaspoons paprika
6 ounces pepperoni sausage, sliced
3 tablespoons chopped fresh parsley
4 cups dried pasta spirals
salt and freshly ground black pepper

1 Chop the onion. Halve and seed the peppers, removing the cores, then cut the flesh into small pieces.

2 Heat the olive oil in a medium saucepan, add the onion and cook for 3 minutes. Stir in the peppers, tomatoes, tomato paste and paprika.

3 Stir the pepperoni into the sauce with 2 tablespoons chopped parsley and a little salt and pepper. Bring to a boil and simmer uncovered for 15–20 minutes, until thickened.

4 Bring a large pan of salted water to a boil, add the pasta and cook for 8–10 minutes, until tender, but not soggy. Drain well. Put the pasta, remaining parsley and a little extra oil in the empty pan and toss together. Divide among warmed bowls and top with the sauce.

Ribbon Noodles with Salsa

Salsa is simply the Spanish word for any kind of sauce.

Serves 2

INGREDIENTS
4 ounces dried ribbon noodles
3 tablespoons olive oil
1 garlic clove, crushed
4 scallions, sliced
3 large tomatoes, chopped
juice of 1 orange
2 tablespoons fresh
    parsley, chopped
salt and freshly ground
    black pepper
cheese, grated, to garnish

1 Bring a pan of salted water to a boil, add the noodles and cook for 8-10 minutes, until they are tender but not soggy. Drain and put in a bowl with a little of the olive oil. Toss the mixture with two forks and season.

2 Heat the remaining oil until it is quite hot and add the garlic and onions. Cook, stirring constantly, for 1 minute. The pan should sizzle.

3 Add the tomatoes, orange juice and parsley. Add some salt and pepper and stir in the noodles to reheat. Serve with the grated cheese.

Stir-fry Rice & Vegetables

Stir-frying is a very quick way of cooking. Stir constantly.

Serves 4

INGREDIENTS
½ cucumber
2 scallions, sliced
1 garlic clove, crushed
2 carrots, thinly sliced
1 small red or yellow bell pepper, seeded
    and sliced
3 tablespoons sunflower or peanut oil
¼ small green cabbage, shredded
generous 4 cups cooked
    long-grain rice
2 tablespoons light soy sauce
1 tablespoon sesame oil
fresh parsley or cilantro, chopped
1 cup unsalted cashews,
    almonds or peanuts
salt and freshly ground black pepper

1 Cut the cucumber in half lengthwise and scoop out the seeds with a teaspoon. Slice the flesh diagonally. Set aside.

2 In a wok or large frying pan, stir-fry the onions, garlic, carrots and pepper in the oil for about 3 minutes, until they are just soft. Add the shredded cabbage and cucumber and stir-fry for 1–2 minutes, until the leaves begin to just wilt. Mix in the rice, soy sauce, sesame oil and a little salt and pepper. Reheat the mixture thoroughly, stirring and tossing constantly.

3 Add the herbs and nuts. Check that there is enough salt and pepper, and serve piping hot.

Tuna & Corn Fish Cakes

Use fresh potatoes, or make a version with instant mashed potatoes.

Serves 4

INGREDIENTS
3½ cups cooked
   mashed potatoes
7-ounce can tuna in
   oil, drained
¾ cup canned or
   frozen corn
2 tablespoons chopped
   fresh parsley
1 cup fresh white or
   brown bread crumbs
salt and freshly ground
   black pepper
lemon and lime wedges,
   to garnish
fresh vegetables, to serve

1 Place the mashed potatoes in a bowl and stir in the tuna, corn and chopped parsley.

2 Add a little salt and pepper, then shape the mixture into eight patties with your hands.

3 Spread out the bread crumbs on a plate and press the fish cakes into the bread crumbs to coat lightly, then place on a baking sheet.

4 Cook the fish cakes under a preheated medium–hot broiler for 7 minutes on each side, until crisp and golden brown. Serve hot with lemon and lime wedges and fresh vegetables.

Jambalaya

This is a quick version of a famous stew from Louisiana. It is just as delicious and very filling.

Serves 4

INGREDIENTS
3 tablespoons vegetable oil
1 medium onion, chopped
1 celery stalk, chopped
½ red bell pepper, seeded
   and chopped
2 cups long-grain rice
4 cups chicken stock
1 tablespoon tomato paste
3–4 shakes of Tabasco sauce
¾ cup frozen peas
8 ounces cold roast chicken
   or pork, thickly sliced
4 ounces cooked sausage,
   such as chorizo sliced

2 Add the rice, chicken stock, tomato paste and Tabasco sauce. Simmer, uncovered, for 10 minutes.

3 Stir in the frozen peas, cold meat and sausage and simmer for another 5 minutes. Switch off the heat, cover and let stand for 5 minutes more before serving.

VARIATION: If desired, you could also add cooked ham, smoked cod or haddock, and cooked shrimp to a Jambalaya.

1 Heat the oil in a heavy saucepan and add the onion, celery and pepper. Cook for 3–5 minutes, to soften without coloring.

Ham & Pineapple French Bread Pizzas

Pizza dough is not difficult to make, but takes quite a long time. French bread makes a great pizza crust and is much quicker.

Serves 4

INGREDIENTS

2 small baguettes
1 jar ready-made thick tomato sauce
3 ounces sliced cooked ham
4 rings canned pineapple, drained well and chopped
½ small green bell pepper, seeded and cut into thin strips
¾ cup Cheddar cheese
salt and freshly ground black pepper

2 Using the back of a spoon, spread the ready-made tomato sauce on the toasted sides of the baguettes until they are evenly covered.

1 Preheat the oven to 400°F, if you are going to bake the pizzas. Cut the baguettes in half lengthwise and toast the cut-sides until crisp and golden.

COOK'S TIP: Most supermarkets sell jars of ready-made tomato sauce for pizza toppings.

3 Cut the slices of cooked ham into strips and arrange the strips on the baguettes with the chopped pineapple and the strips of pepper. Sprinkle with a little salt and pepper.

4 Grate the Cheddar cheese and sprinkle it onto the other topping ingredients on the baguettes.

5 Bake the pizzas or broil them for 15–20 minutes, until they are crisp and golden.

Nachos

This spicy Mexican dish could also be served in taco shells, which, like nachos, are available at most supermarkets.

Serves 4

INGREDIENTS
2 cups ground beef
2 red chiles, seeded and chopped
3 scallions, chopped
6 ounce nacho chips
1¼ cups sour cream
½ cup freshly grated
    Cheddar cheese
salt and freshly ground black pepper

1 Cook the ground beef and chiles in a large pan, without adding any oil, for 10 minutes, stirring constantly.

2 Add the scallions and a little salt and pepper and cook for another 5 minutes. Arrange the nacho chips in four individual flameproof dishes.

3 Spoon on the ground beef mixture and top with sour cream and grated cheese. Broil under medium heat for 5 minutes.

COOK'S TIP: Chiles can burn! Wear rubber gloves and do not touch your face. Take out the fiery seeds with a knife.

Cheese Salad

This salad is full of with vitamins and energy. Serve on slices of crusty bread.

Serves 4

INGREDIENTS

¼ small white cabbage, finely chopped
¼ small red cabbage, finely chopped
8 baby carrots, thinly sliced
¼ cup small mushrooms, quartered
4 ounces cauliflower, cut in small florets
1 small zucchini, grated
4-inch piece cucumber, cubed
2 tomatoes, roughly chopped
2 ounces beans sprouts and chickpeas
½ cup salted peanuts
2 tablespoons sunflower oil
1 tablespoon lemon juice
½ cup grated cheese
salt and freshly ground black pepper

1 Put all the prepared vegetables and the sprouted beans and chickpeas in a bowl and combine.

2 Stir in the peanuts. Drizzle on the oil and the lemon juice. Add a little salt and pepper and let the mixture stand for 30 minutes to let the flavor develop.

3 Sprinkle on the grated cheese just before serving on large slices of crusty bread. Have extra dressing ready, in case anybody wants more.

Fish in Paper Parcels

Wrapping up the fish and vegetables in waxed paper keeps them moist during cooking and makes them fun to serve.

Serves 4

INGREDIENTS
2 tablespoons olive oil
1 onion, thinly sliced
1 garlic clove, finely chopped
1 green bell pepper, seeded and cut into strips
1 red bell pepper, seeded and cut into thin strips
8 ounces tomatoes, coarsely chopped
1 tablespoon chopped fresh mint
2 teaspoons chopped fresh marjoram or
   ½ teaspoon dried oregano
salt and freshly ground black pepper
4 skinless fish fillets, such as flounder or trout
¼ cup feta cheese, crumbled
fresh flat-leaf parsley, to garnish (optional)

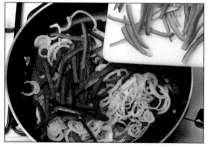

1 Preheat the oven to 350°F. Heat the oil in a frying pan and cook the onion, stirring occasionally, for 3–5 minutes or until soft. Add the garlic and peppers and cook them for 3–5 minutes, until tender, but not browned. Stir in the tomatoes and herbs. Add a little salt and pepper. Remove the pan from heat.

2 Cut four rounds of waxed paper, each the right size to wrap a fish fillet comfortably. Use a large plate as a guide.

3 Put a spoonful of the pepper mixture on one half of each piece of paper and set a fish fillet on top. Spoon some of the remaining pepper mixture on each portion of fish. Sprinkle the cheese on top.

4 Fold the paper over the fish and fold the edges over several times to seal. Put the parcels on a baking sheet.

5 Bake the parcels for 20–25 minutes or until the fish is cooked. Carefully cut the parcels open with scissors, and serve, garnished with flat-leaf parsley, if desired.

COOK'S TIP: To check that the fish is cooked, open the parcels carefully and stick the tip of a knife into the center. The fish should be tender and flaky.

Truly Tropical Kebabs

Chicken goes surprisingly well with fruit, and here it is combined with the slight sharpness of pineapple and the sweetness of banana.

Serves 4

INGREDIENTS
4 boned chicken thighs, skinned and cubed
½ small fresh pineapple
2 firm bananas
freshly cooked rice, to serve
fresh orange wedges and bay leaves,
    to garnish

FOR THE MARINADE
3 tablespoons sunflower oil
1 tablespoon honey
1 teaspoon French
    whole-grain mustard
1 teaspoon crushed coriander seeds
grated zest and juice of
    1 orange
4 cardamom pods

1 Make the marinade. Put the sunflower oil, honey, mustard, coriander seeds, and orange zest and juice in a shallow dish. Mix well to combine. Crush the cardamom pods, extract the seeds and stir them into the mixture.

COOK'S TIP: To check that the chicken is cooked, stick the tip of a knife into the thickest part. The juice should run clear, not pink.

2 Add the prepared chicken cubes to the dish, and turn to coat them all over in the marinade. Then cover the dish and let marinate in the refrigerator for at least 2 hours.

3 Just before cooking, preheat the broiler. Core the pineapple and cut it into neat wedges, leaving the skin on, if desired. Peel and slice the bananas.

4 Add the banana slices and pineapple wedges to the marinade, coating them thoroughly.

5 Drain the chicken, pineapple and banana over a bowl, reserving the marinade. Thread onto eight metal skewers. Place on a broiler rack, under medium heat.

6 Broil for about 15 minutes, turning and brushing with marinade every so often. When the chicken is golden and cooked through, serve on a bed of rice, garnished with orange and bay leaves.

Toad in the Hole

Sausages—not toads—are cooked in a light batter that rises up around them into a crisp, brown crust.

Serves 4

INGREDIENTS
scant 1 cup all-purpose flour
2 tablespoons chopped fresh parsley
2 teaspoons chopped fresh thyme
1 egg, beaten
1¼ cups milk and
    water, mixed
¼ cup oil
1 pound good-quality sausages
salt

1 Stir the flour, herbs and salt together in a bowl and form a well in the center by making a hollow with your hand.

2 Pour the egg into the well, then gradually pour in the milk and water while stirring the dry ingredients into the liquids. Beat to form a smooth batter, then let sit for 30 minutes in the refrigerator.

3 Preheat the oven to 425°F. Pour the oil into a small roasting pan or ovenproof dish, add the sausages and turn them to coat them thoroughly in the oil.

4 Cook the sausages in the oven for 10–15 minutes, until they are beginning to turn brown all over and the oil is very hot.

5 Stir the batter using a wooden spoon, then remove the roasting pan or dish from the oven and quickly pour the batter onto the sausages.

6 Return the pan or dish to the oven to bake for about 40 minutes (depending on the depth of the batter), until well risen and crisp around the edges.

COOK'S TIP: It is important to heat the oil first with the sausages so that the batter rises well and becomes crisp.

Honey Chops

These tasty sticky chops are very quick and easy to prepare and broil, but they would be just as good grilled.

Serves 4

INGREDIENTS
1 pounds carrots
1 tablespoon butter
1 tablespoon brown sugar
1 tablespoon sesame seeds

FOR THE CHOPS
4 pork loin chops
¼ cup butter
2 tablespoons honey
1 tablespoon tomato paste
mashed potatoes, to serve

2 Line the broiler pan with aluminum foil and arrange the pork chops on the broiler rack. Beat the butter and honey together and gradually beat in the tomato paste, to make a smooth paste. Preheat the broiler to high.

1 Cut the carrots into matchstick shapes, put them in a saucepan and just cover them with cold water. Add the butter and brown sugar and bring to a boil. Turn down the heat and let simmer for 15–20 minutes, until most of the liquid has boiled off.

3 Spread half the honey paste on the chops and broiler them for about 5 minutes, until browned.

COOK'S TIP: If the chops are very thick, put under a medium-hot broiler for longer, to make sure they are cooked in the middle.

4 Carefully turn the chops over, spread them with the remaining honey paste and return to the broiler. Broil the second side for another 5 minutes or until the meat is cooked through. Sprinkle the sesame seeds on the carrots and serve with the chops and mashed potatoes.

Cheeseburgers

Nothing beats a homemade burger. Serve with your favorite fries in a lightly toasted bun.

Serves 4

INGREDIENTS
⅓ cup bulghur wheat
2 cups ground beef
1 onion, sliced
1 tablespoon chopped fresh parsley
1 tablespoon tomato paste
1 tablespoon freshly grated
    Parmesan cheese
1 egg, beaten
4 burger buns
lettuce leaves
4 cheese slices
tomato relish
salt and freshly ground black pepper
chips, to serve

1 Place the bulghur wheat in a bowl and add enough boiling water to cover. Let stand for 10 minutes. Drain off any excess liquid if necessary.

2 Preheat the broiler. Put the ground beef into a bowl and break it up with a fork, but do not mash it into a paste.

3 Process the onion and parsley in a food processor for 20 seconds. Add to the beef. Stir in the tomato paste and Parmesan cheese. Add a little salt and pepper. Add the bulghur wheat.

4 Stir in the beaten egg and gather the mixture together into a ball. Shape into four burgers with your hands. Broil for 8–10 minutes on each side under medium heat or until cooked through when pierced with a knife.

COOK'S TIP: Bulghur wheat is also known as cracked wheat. It absorbs water easily and cooks quickly.

5 Split the burger buns in half and toast lightly under the broiler. Place a burger inside each one together with some lettuce leaves. Top with a cheese slice and a spoonful of relish and the burger bun top. Serve with chips and extra relish on the side, if desired.

Eggs Baked in Ham & Hash Potatoes

The eggs nestle attractively in little hollows in the hash, so be careful that you don't break them as you slide them in.

Serves 6

INGREDIENTS
¼ cup butter
1 large onion, chopped
2 cups diced cooked ham
1½ cups diced cooked potatoes
1 cup grated Cheddar cheese
2 tablespoons ketchup
1–2 tablespoons Worcestershire sauce
6 eggs
few drops of Tabasco sauce
salt and freshly ground black pepper
snipped fresh chives, to garnish

1 Preheat the oven to 325°F. Melt half of the butter in a frying pan. Cook the onion until soft, stirring occasionally.

2 Turn the onion into a bowl. Add the ham, potatoes, cheese, ketchup and Worcestershire sauce. Add a little salt and pepper. Stir to combine.

3 Spread the hash in a buttered ovenproof dish in a layer 1 inch deep. Bake for 10 minutes.

4 Make six hollows in the hash mixture. Carefully slide an egg into each of the hollows.

COOK'S TIP: It is better to break each egg into a small bowl first, so that you can take out any pieces of shell before sliding the egg into the hash.

5 Melt the remaining butter in a small pan. Season with Tabasco sauce to taste. Drizzle the seasoned butter on the eggs and hash.

6 Bake for 15–20 minutes or until the eggs are set and cooked to your taste. Serve immediately, in the dish, garnished with chives.

Crêpe Parcels

Be creative with your crêpes! Try this savory version for a real change.

Serves 4

INGREDIENTS
1 cup all-purpose flour
1 egg
1¼ cups milk
½ teaspoon salt
2 tablespoons butter, for frying
scallions, blanched, to garnish (optional)

FOR THE FILLING
scant 1 cup cream cheese
    with chives
6 tablespoons heavy cream
4 ounces ham, cut in strips
1 cup cheese, grated
¼ cup fresh bread crumbs
salt and freshly ground black pepper

1 To make the crêpes, put the flour, egg, a little milk and the salt in a bowl and beat together with a wooden spoon. Gradually beat in the rest of the milk until the batter looks like heavy cream. (The milk must be added slowly or the batter will be lumpy.)

2 Melt a little butter in a medium-size frying pan and pour in just enough batter to cover the bottom in a thin layer. Tilt and turn the pan to spread the batter out. Cook gently until set, then turn over with a spatula and cook the second side. If you feel brave enough, try tossing the crêpes!

3 Slide the crêpe out of the pan. There should be enough batter to make four large crêpes. Stack them in a pile, with a piece of waxed paper between each one to keep them from sticking to each other. Preheat the oven to 375°F.

4 Make the filling. Beat the cream cheese and cream in a bowl. Add the ham and half the cheese and stir in a little salt and pepper. Put a spoonful of the mixture in the center of a crêpe.

5 Fold one side over the mixture and then the other. Fold both ends up as well to make a small parcel.

6 Arrange the parcels on a baking sheet, with the seams underneath. Make three more parcels in the same way. Sprinkle the remaining cheese and the bread crumbs on the parcels and cover with aluminum foil. Cook for 20 minutes. Remove the foil. Cook for 10 more minutes, until browned. Tie green scallions around the parcels, if desired.

Falafel

A Middle Eastern street snack!

Makes 8

INGREDIENTS
15-ounce can chickpeas, drained
1 garlic clove, crushed
2 tablespoons chopped fresh parsley
2 tablespoons chopped cilantro
1 tablespoon chopped fresh mint
1 teaspoon cumin seeds
2 tablespoons fresh bread crumbs
freshly ground black pepper
oil, for frying

TO SERVE
pita bread, warmed
lettuce and tomatoes
Hummus or plain yogurt

1 Grind the drained chickpeas in a food processor until they are just smooth, then mix them with all the other ingredients except the oil, until you have a thick, creamy paste. Add pepper to taste.

2 Using wet hands, shape the chickpea mixture into eight balls and chill for 30 minutes so they become firm.

3 Meanwhile, heat about ¼ inch of oil in a shallow frying pan and fry the falafels a few at a time. Cook for about 8 minutes, turning just once. Drain on paper towels and reheat the oil between batches. Serve in pita bread with salad and Hummus or yogurt.

Caribbean Rice

This dish is very tasty and healthy.

Serves 4

INGREDIENTS
generous 1 cup long-grain rice
14-ounce can kidney beans
3 cups water
2 ounces coconut, milk
1 teaspoon dried thyme or
    1 tablespoon fresh thyme leaves
1 small onion stuck with 6 whole cloves
salt and freshly ground black pepper

1 Put the rice and kidney beans into a large saucepan with the rest of the ingredients.

2 Bring to a boil, stirring until smooth. Cover and simmer gently for 20 minutes.

3 Remove the lid and let cook, uncovered, for 5 minutes, to reduce any excess liquid. Remove from heat and stir occasionally to separate the grains. Remove the onion and serve.

Right: Falafel (top); Caribbean Rice

Let's Get Tropical

Supermarkets are full of wonderful fruits that make a really delicious when combined. Serve with cream or yogurt.

Serves 4

INGREDIENTS
1 small pineapple
2 kiwi fruits
1 ripe mango
1 slice watermelon
2 peaches
2 bananas
¼ cup tropical fruit juice

1 Cut the pineapple into ½-inch slices. Work around the edge of each slice, cutting off the skin and any spiky pieces. Remove the cores, cut each slice into wedges and put them in a bowl.

2 Use a potato peeler to remove the skin from the kiwi fruit. Cut them in half lengthwise and then into wedges. Add to the fruit bowl.

3 Cut the mango lengthwise into quarters and cut around the large flat pit. Peel the flesh and cut it into chunks or slices.

4 Cut the watermelon into slices, cut off the skin and cut the flesh into chunks. Remove the seeds. Cut the peaches in half, remove the pits and cut the flesh into wedges. Slice the bananas. Add all the fruit to the bowl and gently stir in the fruit juice.

Chocolate & Banana Dip

Malted drinks and "smoothies" are very popular, and this delectable dip is great served with chunks of fresh fruit.

Serves 4

INGREDIENTS
2 ounces bittersweet chocolate
2 large ripe bananas
1 tablespoon malt extract

1 Break the chocolate into pieces and place in a small heatproof bowl. Stand the bowl over a pan of gently simmering water and stir the chocolate occasionally until it melts. Do not let the bottom of the bowl touch the water. Let cool.

2 Cut the bananas into pieces and process them until finely chopped in a blender or food processor.

3 With the motor running, pour in the malt extract, and continue processing until the mixture is thick and frothy.

4 Drizzle in the chocolate in a steady stream and process until well blended. Serve immediately.

Crispy Cinnamon Toasts

You can use fancy cutters to create an eye-catching dessert or, if you do not have cutters, simply cut the crusts off the bread and cut into little fingers.

Serves 4

INGREDIENTS
2 ounces raisins
3 tablespoons orange juice
4 medium slices white bread
3 small eggs, beaten
1 tablespoon ground cinnamon
2 large oranges
1½ tablespoons sunflower oil
2 tablespoons unsalted butter
1 tablespoon sugar
thick plain yogurt, to serve

1 Put the raisins in a small bowl and add the orange juice. Let soak for 10 minutes, so that they plump up and absorb the flavor of the juice.

2 Cut the bread into shapes with a cutter. Place the shapes in a bowl with the eggs and cinnamon to soak.

3 Peel the oranges. Remove any excess pith from the peel, then cut the peel into fine strips and cook in boiling water for 2 minutes. Refresh it in cold water, then drain.

4 Strain the raisins. Heat a wok or frying pan, then add the oil. When the oil is hot, stir in the butter until melted, then add the bread and fry, turning once, until golden brown. Stir in the raisins and orange zest, and sprinkle with sugar. Serve warm with thick yogurt.

Peach Melba

The original dish created for the opera singer Dame Nellie Melba had peaches and ice cream served upon an ice swan.

Serves 4

INGREDIENTS
scant 2 cups raspberries
squeeze of lemon juice
confectioners' sugar, to taste
15-ounce can sliced peaches
8 scoops vanilla ice cream

1 Press the raspberries through a nonmetallic sieve to make a purée and remove the seeds.

2 Add a little lemon juice to the raspberry purée and sweeten to taste with confectioners' sugar.

3 Transfer the peaches to a sieve and drain thoroughly.

4 Place two scoops of ice cream in each individual glass dish, top with peach slices, then pour on the raspberry purée. Serve immediately.

Strawberry & Apple Crumble

Raspberries can be used instead of strawberries, either fresh or frozen. Serve warm, with custard or yogurt.

Serves 4

INGREDIENTS
1 pound cooking apples
1¼ cups strawberries
2 tablespoons sugar
½ teaspoon ground cinnamon
2 tablespoons orange juice
custard or plain yogurt,
    to serve

FOR THE CRUMBLE
3 tablespoons whole-wheat flour
⅔ cup oats
2 tablespoons butter

2 Toss together the apples, strawberries, sugar, cinnamon and orange juice. Transfer to a 5-cup ovenproof dish, or four individual dishes.

3 Combine the flour and oats in a bowl and then mix in the butter with a fork until combined and crumbly.

1 Preheat the oven to 350°F. Peel, core and slice the apples. Hull and halve the strawberries.

VARIATION: For a change, you might like to replace some of the oats in the crumble with some chopped mixed nuts.

4 Sprinkle the crumble evenly onto the fruit. Bake for 40–45 minutes (20–25 minutes for individual dishes), until golden brown and bubbling. Serve the crumble warm, with custard or yogurt.

Pineapple & Strawberry Pavlova

This pavlova doesn't usually hold a perfect shape, but it has a wonderful texture.

Serves 6

INGREDIENTS
5 egg whites, at room temperature
pinch of salt
1 teaspoon cornstarch
1 tablespoon vinegar
few drops of vanilla extract
1½ cups sugar
1 cup whipping
    cream, whipped
6 ounces fresh pineapple,
    cut into chunks
6 ounces fresh strawberries, halved
strawberry leaves, to decorate (optional)

1 Preheat the oven to 325°F. Line a baking sheet with nonstick baking parchment.

3 Gently whisk in half the sugar, then carefully fold in the rest, stirring gently in a figure-eight until all the sugar is mixed into the meringue.

4 Spoon the meringue onto the baking sheet and swirl into an 8-inch round with the back of a large spoon. Make a hollow in the center for the fruit and cream.

2 Put the egg whites in a large bowl and whisk until they form stiff peaks. Add the salt, cornstarch, vinegar and vanilla; whisk again until stiff.

5 Bake for 20 minutes, then reduce the oven temperature to 300°F and bake the meringue for another 40 minutes.

6 Transfer to a serving plate while still warm, then let cool. When ready to serve, fill with whipped cream, chunks of pineapple and halved strawberries. Decorate with strawberry leaves, if you have them.

COOK'S TIP: You can also cook this in a deep, 8-inch loose-bottomed cake pan. Cover the bottom with nonstick baking parchment and grease the sides with a little butter.

Rustic Apple Pie

You don't need to be extra careful when making this rustic pie, as it looks best when it's really craggy and rough. Serve with whipped cream or custard.

Serves 6

INGREDIENTS
2 cups all-purpose flour
1 tablespoon sugar
1 tablespoon ground allspice
$\frac{2}{3}$ cup butter or margarine
1 egg, separated
1 pounds apples
2 tablespoons lemon juice
$\frac{1}{2}$ cup sugar
$\frac{2}{3}$ cup raisins
$\frac{1}{4}$ cup hazelnuts, toasted
    and chopped

2 Transfer to a lightly floured surface and knead gently until smooth. Roll out to make a circle about 12 inches across. Use the rolling pin to lift the pastry onto a small baking sheet. It should hang over the edges.

1 Put the flour, sugar and allspice in a bowl and stir. Add the butter or margarine and rub it into the flour with your fingertips, until the mixture looks like bread crumbs. Add the egg yolk and use your hands to pull the mixture together to make the pastry. You may need to add a little water.

3 Peel and slice the apples. Toss them in the lemon juice, to keep them from turning brown. Place some on the middle of the pastry, leaving a 4-inch border all around. Reserve 2 tablespoons of the sugar. Sprinkle some of the raisins on top, then add some of the remaining sugar. Keep making layers of apples, raisins and sugar until you have used them up.

4 Preheat the oven to 400°F. Fold up the pastry to cover most of the fruit, overlapping where needed. Don't worry about neatness.

5 Brush with egg white and sprinkle on the reserved sugar. Sprinkle on the nuts. Cover the hole with aluminum foil to keep the raisins from burning. Cook for 30–35 minutes, until the pastry is cooked and browned.

Peanut Butter Cookies

These scrumptious cookies are very easy to make—the worst thing is waiting for them to cool before you can eat them.

Makes 24

INGREDIENTS
1 cup all-purpose flour
½ teaspoon baking soda
½ teaspoon salt
½ cup butter, at room temperature
¾ cup light brown sugar
1 egg
1 teaspoon vanilla extract
1 cup crunchy peanut butter

1 Sift together the flour, baking soda and salt into a bowl and set aside. With an electric mixer, cream the butter and sugar together until light and fluffy.

2 In another bowl, mix the egg and vanilla, then gradually beat into the butter mixture. Stir in the peanut butter and mix thoroughly. Stir in the dry ingredients. for at least 30 minutes or until firm.

3 Preheat the oven to 350°F. Grease two baking sheets. Spoon out rounded teaspoonfuls of the dough and roll into balls. Place the balls on the prepared sheets and press flat with a fork into circles about 2½ inches in diameter, making a criss-cross pattern. Bake for 12–15 minutes, until lightly colored. Transfer to a rack to cool.

Raspberry Muffins

These muffins are made using baking powder and buttermilk, giving them a light and spongy texture—delicious at any time of day!

Makes 10–12

INGREDIENTS
2½ cups all-purpose flour
1 tablespoon baking powder
½ cup sugar
1 egg
1 cup buttermilk or milk
¼ cup sunflower oil
scant 1 cup raspberries

1 Preheat the oven to 400°F. Arrange 12 paper cases in a deep muffin pan. Sift the flour and baking powder into a mixing bowl, stir in the sugar, then make a well in the center.

2 Combine the egg, buttermilk or milk and sunflower oil in a bowl, pour into the flour mixture and mix quickly until just combined.

3 Add the raspberries and lightly fold in with a metal spoon, stirring in a figure-eight movement. Spoon the mixture into the paper cases to within a third of the top.

4 Bake for 20–25 minutes, until the muffins are golden brown and firm in the middle. Transfer to a wire rack and serve warm or cold.

Fruity Muesli Bars

These fruity muesli bars are an appetizing treat.

Makes 10–12

INGREDIENTS
½ cup butter or margarine,
  plus extra for greasing
⅓ cup light brown sugar
3 tablespoons light corn syrup
1¼ cups Swiss-style muesli
½ cup rolled oats
1 teaspoon ground allspice
⅓ cup golden raisins
½ cup dried pears, chopped

3 Remove the pan from heat, add the muesli, oats, allspice, golden raisins and pears and mix well.

1 Preheat the oven to 350°F. Lightly grease 7-inch square cake pan.

2 Put the butter or margarine, sugar and syrup in a saucepan and gently heat, stirring constantly with a wooden spoon, until melted and blended.

4 Transfer the mixture to the prepared pan and level the surface, pressing down.

5 Bake for 20–30 minutes, until golden brown. Cool slightly in the pan, then cut the mixture into bars using a sharp knife.

VARIATION: Just rolled oats can be used instead of the Swiss-style muesli, if desired.

6 When firm, remove the muesli bars from the pan and place them on a wire rack to cool.

COOK'S TIP: These bars will keep better if stored in an airtight container—that is, if there are any left at all!

Carrot Cake

This is full of healthy fiber—yet is moist and soft and tastes delicious.

Serves 10–12

INGREDIENTS
2 cups self-rising flour
2 teaspoons baking powder
scant 1 cup brown sugar
4 ounces dried figs,
    roughly chopped
8 ounces carrots, grated
2 small ripe bananas, mashed
2 eggs
⅔ cup sunflower oil
¾ cup cream cheese
1½ cups confectioners' sugar, sifted
colored sprinkles, nuts or
    grated chocolate, to decorate

1 Lightly grease a 7-inch round springform cake pan. Cut a piece of baking parchment or waxed paper to fit the bottom of the pan.

2 Preheat the oven to 350°F. Put the flour, baking powder and sugar into a large bowl and mix well. Stir in the figs.

3 Using your hands, squeeze as much liquid out of the grated carrots as you can and add them to the bowl. Mix in the mashed bananas.

4 Beat the eggs and oil together and pour them into the mixture. Beat together with a wooden spoon.

5 Spoon into the prepared pan and level the top. Cook for 1–1¼ hours, until a skewer pushed into the center of the cake comes out clean. Remove the cake from the pan and let cool on a wire rack.

6 Beat the cream cheese and confectioners' sugar together, to make a thick icing. Spread it on top of the cake. Decorate with colored sprinkles, nuts or grated chocolate. Cut in small wedges, to serve, or store for up to a week.

This edition published by Southwater

Distributed in the UK by
The Manning Partnership, 251-253 London Road East,
Batheaston, Bath BA1 7RL, UK
tel. (0044) 01225 852 727 fax. (0044) 01225 852 852

Distributed in the USA by
Ottenheimer Publishing, 5 Park Center Court,
Suite 300, Owing Mills MD 2117-5001, USA
tel. (001) 410 902 9100 fax. (001) 410 902 7210

Distributed in Australia by
Sandstone Publishing, Unit 1, 360 Norton Street,
Leichhardt, New South Wales 2040, Australia
tel. (0061) 2 9560 7888 fax. (0061) 2 9560 7488

Distributed in New Zealand by
Five Mile Press NZ, PO Box 33-1071,
Takapuna, Auckland 9, New Zealand
tel. (0064) 9 4444 144 fax. (0064) 9 4444 518

Southwater is an imprint of Anness Publishing Limited

© 2000 Anness Publishing Limited

Publisher: Joanna Lorenz
Editor: Valerie Ferguson
Series Designer: Bobbie Colgate Stone
Designer: Andrew Heath
Editorial Reader: Kate Henderson
Production Controller: Joanna King

Recipes contributed by: Alex Barker, Maxine
Clarke, Roz Denny, Christine France,
Silvano Franco, Shirley Gill, Carole Handslip,
Patricia Lousada, Norma MacMillan,
Maggie Pannell, Anne Sheasby,
Jenny Stacey, Liz Trigg, Hilaire Walden,
Steven Wheeler, Judy Williams.

Photography: Karl Adamson, Edward Allwright,
Steve Baxter, James Duncan, Michelle Garrett,
Amanda Heywood, David Jordan, Don Last,
William Lingwood, Michael Michaels.

A CIP catalogue record for this book
is available from the British Library.

1 3 5 7 9 10 8 6 4 2

Printed and bound in Singapore

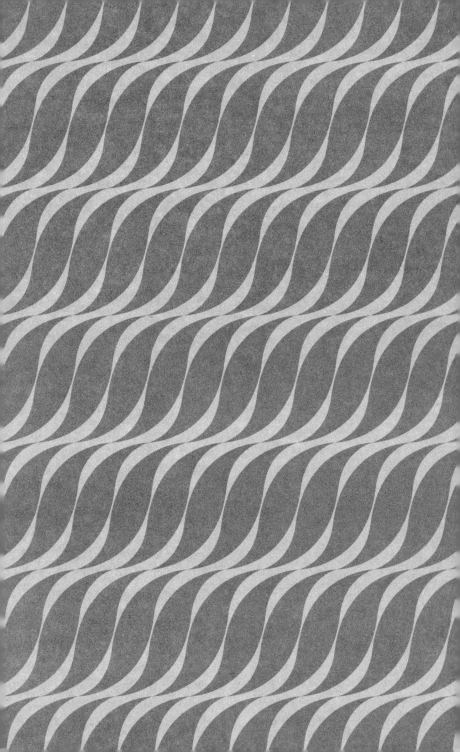